The Navajo Nation

by Sandra M. Pasqua

Consultant:
Steven Begay
Navajo Cultural Specialist
Traditional Culture Program
Navajo Nation Historic Preservation Department

Bridgestone Books
an imprint of Capstone Press
Mankato, Minnesota

Bridgestone Books are published by Capstone Press
151 Good Counsel Drive, P.O. Box 669, Mankato, Minnesota 56002
http://www.capstone-press.com

Library of Congress Cataloging-in-Publication Data
Pasqua, Sandra M.
    The Navajo Nation/by Sandra M. Pasqua.
        p. cm.—(Native peoples)
    Includes bibliographical references and index.
    Summary: A history of the largest group of Native Americans in the United States and
a description of their homes, educational system, government, ceremonies, stories, location,
and their role as codetalkers.
    ISBN 0-7368-0499-4
    1. Navajo Indians—History—Juvenile literature. 2. Navajo Indians—Social life and
customs—Juvenile literature. [1. Navajo Indians. 2. Indians of North America—Southwest,
New.] I. Title. II. Series.
E99.N3 P376 2000
979.1'004972—dc21

                                                                                    99-052187

Editorial Credits
Rebecca Glaser, editor; Timothy Halldin, cover designer and illustrator; Sara A. Sinnard,
    illustrator; Kimberly Danger and Katy Kudela, photo researchers

Photo Credits
Corbis, 14
Denise Oldham, cover, 6, 8
Don Eastman, 16
John Elk III, 12
Marilyn "Angel" Wynn, 10
Timothy Begay, 18
Tom Till, 20

1 2 3 4 5 6 05 04 03 02 01 00

Table of Contents

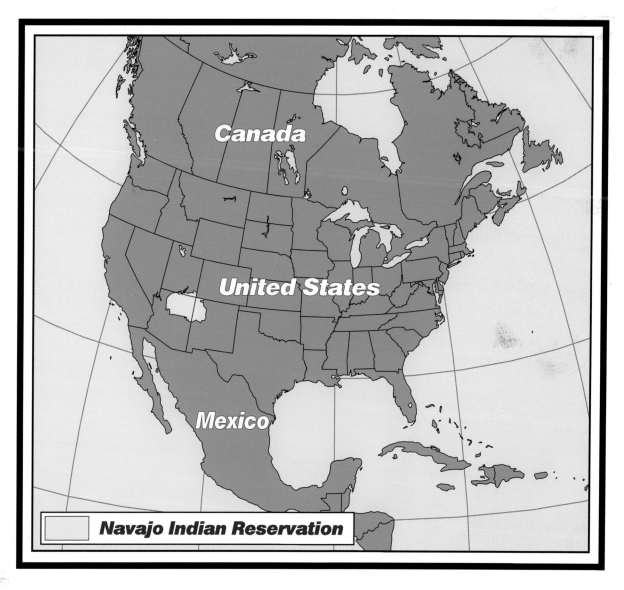

The Navajo live in the southwestern United States. Most Navajo people live on the Navajo Indian Reservation. The reservation covers parts of Arizona, Utah, and New Mexico.

Fast Facts

The Navajo (NAH-vuh-hoh) Nation is the largest group of Native Americans in the United States. Navajo people call themselves Diné (dee-NEY), which means "the people" in the Navajo language. These facts tell about the Navajo in the past and today.

Homes: Traditional Navajo homes are called hogans. A hogan is a dome-shaped, one-room building. The Navajo make hogans from logs. They cover the roof with thick mud. Today, the Navajo often live in modern houses. Many Navajo families also have a hogan.

Food: In the past, the Navajo grew corn, squash, and beans. Corn was an important Navajo food. The Navajo also raised animals for food.

Clothing: Long ago, Navajo women made clothes from animal skins for their families. Later, the Navajo learned to weave sheep's wool into rugs, blankets, and cloth for clothes. Today, the Navajo wear both traditional and modern clothes.

Language: The Navajo language comes from the Athabascan group of languages. Many Navajo still speak the language today.

The Navajo Nation

The Navajo call themselves Diné. This word means "the people" in their language.

Spanish explorers gave the Diné the name Navajo hundreds of years ago. The Navajo lived in the southwestern United States near the Pueblo Indians. The Tewa group of Pueblo called their neighbors "Nabahu," which means "planted fields." Spanish explorers came to the Southwest in the 1500s. The Spanish heard the Tewa word and called the Diné "Navajo." In 1969, the Navajo decided to call their tribe the Navajo Nation.

The Navajo Indian Reservation is located where Arizona, New Mexico, Utah, and Colorado meet. This reservation is the largest Native American reservation in the United States. The reservation covers 25,000 square miles (64,750 square kilometers). This area is about the size of West Virginia.

Most young Navajo people live on the reservation today.

The Navajo People

About 250,000 people make up the Navajo Nation. Most Navajo people live on the reservation.

Navajos are born into a large extended family called a clan. Navajo clans are matrilineal. Members of the clan are related through their mother's family. When a Navajo man marries, he lives with his wife's clan. Clan members often live in the same area. Today, the Navajo Nation has more than 65 clans.

In the past, the Navajo farmed and raised livestock. Today, some Navajos still are farmers or ranchers. They raise sheep, cattle, horses, and goats.

Some Navajos make a living from crafts. Navajo women weave colorful blankets and rugs from dyed sheep's wool. Other artists on the reservation make silver and turquoise jewelry.

The Navajo have other jobs as well. Many Navajos work for the Navajo government as teachers, police officers, or in other official jobs.

Some Navajos raise sheep for a living.

Hogans

A hogan is a traditional Navajo home. A hogan is a dome-shaped, one-room building. A hogan has a fireplace in the center of the floor. The home has one door that faces east to welcome the rising sun.

The Navajo built the first hogans with four beams propped against each other. They then covered this frame with brush and mud. These cone-shaped hogans were called forked-stick hogans.

Later, the Navajo built hogans with logs placed in a circular or octagonal shape. Mud that covered the roof became hard after it baked in the sun.

Navajo families preferred to be outside during the summer. A family might move to a ramada. The Navajo built this open-sided shelter with tree branches. The family returned to the hogan when the weather cooled.

Today, most Navajo live in modern houses and also have a hogan. They use hogans for ceremonies. Some families on the reservation still live in hogans.

Typical Navajo hogans are dome-shaped and have a door that faces east.

Navajo Education

In the early 1900s, the U.S. government forced many Navajo children to attend boarding schools. The children lived at schools far away from their homes. They did not see their families often.

In 1950, the United States Congress passed a law to help the Navajo. The law provided money to help the Navajo build public schools on the reservation. Today, Navajo children go to local schools managed by the Navajo government.

The Navajo opened the first Native American college in the United States. Navajo Community College was established in 1968. Classes began in 1969. The Navajo Nation runs the college. Today, the college is called Diné College. In 1974, a main campus opened in Tsaile, Arizona. Today, the college also has small campuses in other towns on the reservation. Both Navajo and non-Navajo students attend Diné College.

The Ned A. Hatathli Center at Diné College was built in the octagonal shape of a hogan.

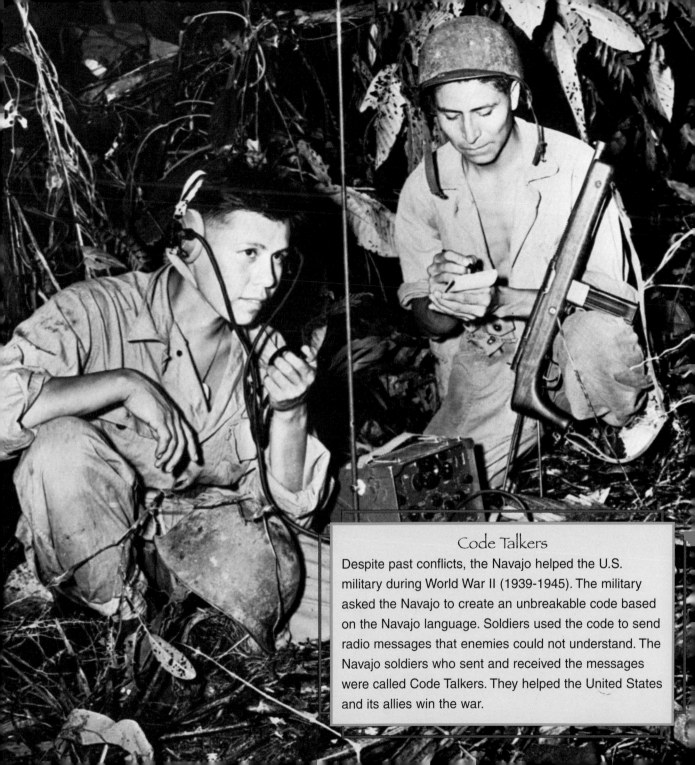

Code Talkers

Despite past conflicts, the Navajo helped the U.S. military during World War II (1939-1945). The military asked the Navajo to create an unbreakable code based on the Navajo language. Soldiers used the code to send radio messages that enemies could not understand. The Navajo soldiers who sent and received the messages were called Code Talkers. They helped the United States and its allies win the war.

Navajo History

In the 1800s, many European settlers wanted to live on Navajo land. The U.S. government wanted to stop the Navajo from fighting with settlers. In 1863, the U.S. Army sent Colonel Christopher "Kit" Carson to remove the Navajo from their land.

Carson and his men destroyed Navajo animals and crops. In 1864, Carson forced 8,000 Navajo to walk nearly 350 miles (560 kilometers) to Fort Sumner. The Navajo call this journey the "Long Walk." Many Navajo died. Those who survived were prisoners for four years.

The U.S. government wanted to open the West to settlers. Officials wanted to make peace with Native Americans. The U.S. government gave the Navajo the choice of moving to Indian Territory in Oklahoma or to their homeland. The Navajo chose to move back to the Southwest. In 1868, the Navajo signed a treaty with the U.S. government. This treaty established the Navajo Indian Reservation. The land was only part of the Navajo homeland.

Navajo Government

In the past, the Navajo did not have a central government. Each clan had a headman who made decisions. In 1921, oil was discovered on the Navajo reservation. The Navajo needed a central government to make deals for the whole nation.

In 1923, the Navajo elected a Tribal Council. The council had 12 people who made decisions for the Navajo Nation. In 1927, the Navajo organized local governments. Communities formed chapters. The chapters elected leaders to represent them at Tribal Council meetings. Today, there are 110 chapters.

The Navajo Nation has the largest government on a Native American reservation. In 1991, the government created executive, legislative, and judicial branches. The president and vice president are the executive branch. The legislative branch has 88 delegates from the chapters. The court system is the judicial branch. The government meets in Window Rock, Arizona.

Window Rock, Arizona, is the capital of the Navajo Nation. The town is named for a rock formation that looks like a large window.

Creation Story

The Navajo creation story tells of four worlds. The first world is the black world, or dark world. Insects live there. The second world is the blue world. Blue jays, blue birds, and blue hawks live there. The third world is the yellow world. Larger animals such as squirrels and turkeys live there. The fourth world is the glittering world. The Navajo live in this world.

First Man and First Woman travel through the worlds with the animals. In the fourth world, they find a baby girl and care for her. The girl goes through the first Kinaalda ceremony. She grows up to be Changing Woman.

Changing Woman has twin sons, fathered by the Sun. They are Child Born of Water and Monster Slayer. The twins save the world from monsters. Changing Woman goes to live with the Sun. She becomes lonely for her children. She makes four sets of people called the water clan people. The Navajo are descended from many clans, including the water clan people.

The Holy People created four sacred mountains that form the boundaries of Navajo land. The eastern mountain, Sisnaajini, stands in southern Colorado.

Ceremonies

Hataałii are Navajo singers who perform ceremonies. The singers know the songs and prayers that are part of each ceremony.

The Navajo have ceremonies for many parts of their lives. The Blessingway ceremony is performed to bring harmony to a person's life. This ceremony is part of all other Navajo ceremonies. Navajo girls go through a ceremony called Kinaalda. After this ceremony, girls are considered women. The Navajo also have ceremonies for events such as childbirth, blessing a new hogan, healing, and other events.

The Navajo use sandpaintings in ceremonies for healing or health. During the ceremony, a singer uses powdered rock to make the sandpainting. The sandpainting summons the Holy People to the hogan. The Holy People are Navajo gods. Navajos ask the Holy People for help in healing. The singer destroys the sandpainting when the ceremony is done.

Sandpaintings summon the Holy People to a hogan.

Hands On: Tsindł

Navajo people of all ages play Tsindł (SIN-dilth). This game teaches Navajo children about the boundaries of their land. It also teaches them to count.

What You Need

3 wooden craft sticks
Black permanent marker
Flat rock about 6 inches
    (15 centimeters) wide
40 pebbles
A pencil or pen for each player

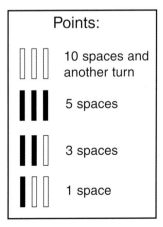

What You Do

1. Color one side of each craft stick black. The craft sticks are dice.
2. Place the rock in the center of the playing area with the flat side up. The rock represents the sun.
3. Divide the pebbles into four sets of 10. Place the pebbles in a circle like the diagram above. After every 10 pebbles, leave a gap for each of the four directions. The gaps represent the rivers that border Navajo land.
4. All players place their pencils at the first pebble after the East gap.
5. The first player holds the three sticks vertically and bounces them off the rock at the same time.
6. Count your points by how the dice land (see chart). Move your pencil to that pebble.
7. If a player lands on your pencil, you must go back to the beginning of the section.
8. Each river is a space. If you land in a river, you must go back to the beginning of the section.
9. The first player to get around all 40 pebbles wins.

Points:	
|||	10 spaces and another turn
▮▮▮	5 spaces
▮▮|	3 spaces
▮||	1 space

Words to Know

campus (KAM-puhss)—the land and buildings of a college

chapter (CHAP-tuhr)—a local Navajo community

delegate (DEL-uh-guht)—a person who represents other people at a meeting

Diné (dee-NEY)—a Navajo word that means "the people"

hogan (HOH-guhn)—a traditional Navajo home

matrilineal (MAH-truh-lin-ee-uhl)—descending from the mother

octagonal (ok-TAG-uh-nuhl)—having eight sides

reservation (res-uhr-VAY-shuhn)—land owned and controlled by Native Americans

summon (SUHM-uhn)—to call or request someone to come

Read More

Abbink, Emily. *Colors of the Navajo.* Colors of the World. Minneapolis: Carolrhoda Books, 1998.

Begay, Shonto. *Navajo: Visions and Voices across the Mesa.* New York: Scholastic, 1995.

Hucko, Bruce. *A Rainbow at Night: The World in Words and Pictures by Navajo Children.* San Francisco: Chronicle Books, 1996.

Thomson, Peggy. *Katie Henio, Navajo Sheepherder.* New York: Cobblehill Books/Dutton, 1995.

Useful Addresses

**Navajo Nation Historic
   Preservation Department**
Traditional Culture Program
P.O. Box 4950
Window Rock, AZ 86515

Navajo Tribal Museum
P.O. Box 9000
Window Rock, AZ 86515

Internet Sites

Navajo Central
http://navajocentral.org
The Navajo Nation
http://www.navajo.org
Navajos.com
http://www.navajos.com

Index